First edition published 2024
Copyright © 2024 by Katie H Publishing

All rights reserved. No part of this publication may be reproduced, distributed, or transmitted in any form or by any means, including photocopying, recording, or other electronic or mechanical methods, without the prior written permission of the publisher. For permission requests, write to the publisher, addressed "Attention: Permissions Coordinator," at the address below.

Apple Tree Cottage
5 The Mead
Clutton
Bristol
England
BS39 5RF

© Collecting Moments is a Trademark of Katie H Publishing
2024

Cover design by © Katie H Publishing
Cover elements under licence from Canva.com
Internal design by © Katie H Publishing
Internal elements under licence from Canva.com

Medical Disclaimer

Last updated 16th April, 2024.

This book 'Collect Moments Not Things' details the author's personal experiences with and opinions about living more gratefully, for a happier, more enriched life. The author Katie H is not a healthcare provider.

The author and publisher are providing this book 'Collect Moments Not Things' and its contents on an "as is" basis and make no representations or guarantees of any kind with respect to this book or its contents. The author and publisher disclaim all such representations and guarantees, including for example warranties of merchantability and healthcare for a particular purpose. In addition, the author and publisher do not represent or guarantee that the information accessible via this book 'Collect Moments Not Things' is accurate, complete or current.

Except as specifically stated in this book 'Collect Moments Not Things', neither the author or publisher, nor any authors, contributors, or other representatives will be liable for damages arising out of or in connection with the use of this book 'Collect Moments Not Things'. This is a comprehensive limitation of liability that applies to all damages of any kind, including (without limitation) compensatory; direct, indirect or consequential damages; loss of data, income or profit; loss of or damage to property and claims of third parties.

You understand that this book 'Collect Moments Not Things' is not intended as a substitute for consultation with a licensed healthcare practitioner, such as your General Practitioner. Before you begin any healthcare program, or change your lifestyle in any way, you will consult your doctor or another licensed healthcare practitioner to ensure that you are in good health and that the examples contained in this book 'Collect Moments Not Things' will not harm you.

This book 'Collect Moments Not Things' provides content related to mental health issues. As such, use of this book implies your acceptance of this disclaimer.

Collect Moments Not Things

I dedicate Collect Moments Not Things to my Daughters R and V, whose love and support have got me through some of the most challenging years of my life. I don't know how I could have done it without you.

Here's to you, 'Princess Fluff-Much' and 'Poppetty' (they will disown me for that)!

CONTENTS

Part One
Nuts & Bolts---------------- Page 01

Please don't skip this as it's integral to the book!

Part Two
Exercises & Examples---- Page 14

Part Three
Gratitude & Goodness---- Page 22

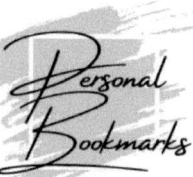

Personal Bookmarks

Page		Page	

Many men and women understand how easily life can become hectic, stressful, and busy. We are overcommitted, have no free time, feel we need more money, and feel trapped in the daily demands of life. But the good news is: you don't have to live this way!

When I was a child, we rented the second floor of a large Victorian house. We had only two tiny bedrooms, one lounge, a small kitchen, and a shared toilet - no bathroom, for a family of four. That is how we lived until I was eleven when my parents managed to secure a council house. There were no savings, designer clothes, luxuries, cars, fancy food on the table, dining out at restaurants, no Netflix, no social media, and you counted yourself as lucky if your holidays were spent caravanning in Wales for a week! Sounds depressing, doesn't it. But that is how it was. We all accepted it. What was marvellous about those times was that life was slower, much less competitive, and less complicated; you couldn't send a quick Snapchat to your friends, so people found more time for each other face-to-face.

Happiness is also relative to your circumstances. If you spent eleven or twelve hours of every day working in a factory or out in the fields, then it wouldn't take that much to give you a feeling of happiness - a single beer to be savoured watching the sunset, a smile and a wave from a passing friend; countless things that we would today, see as mundane could have brought people great happiness in more difficult times. A case, in fact, is during those times before my family secured the council house, my idea of heaven was lying in front of the electric bar heater on the only rug we owned, watching The Avengers on the black and white television and eating a jam sandwich; I kid you not! Christmas was magical, but it could not compare to how many presents children get nowadays. We each got one pillowcase filled with small gifts, tangerines and nuts and thought we were the luckiest children alive. Yes, you read that correctly - one pillowcase.

Fast forward to the present day. What do we have? We have more in the way of consumer benefits. We have more opportunity. More money in our pockets. More things to spend that money on. We have more choices. We also have more competitiveness, and we have a generation of young people under immense pressure to perform, to be the best they can be, and to be on the side of the 'have's' rather than the 'have nots'. Expectation levels have increased exponentially in today's modern society. Our lives are crammed with commitments and fast-paced lifestyles. It's all very overwhelming and exhausting. The majority are in a race to compete and outdo one another. We're using stress and greed as motivators instead of love. This is putting us in constant fight or flight mode. We're acting irrationally, filling our lives with needless luxuries and distractions, processed foods, social media, artificial lights, noise, and pollution instead of appreciating the finer things, the natural things we have for free but often take for granted. It's making us feel like we must keep up to avoid feeling inferior or inadequate. This has led to more mental health issues, more alcohol and drug abuse, more depression, and more anxiety. You only have to see the statistics of anti-depressant usage, the proliferation of psychotherapists and counsellors, and the rise in suicide rates to understand the difference between past generations and now.

But I'm not here to depress you, my friend. Having this book in your hands means you instinctively know something is wrong and want to fix it. So this is the good news: It **can** be fixed, and you can lead a happier life if you allow me to take your hand and lead you in the right direction.

At its core, this journal is a tool for self-discovery. It's a safe space, a sanctuary where you can build a collection of memories and dreams—a place where you can truly be yourself. It's a source of comfort, and love—so much more than just a journal.

Sometimes being grateful means choosing to see what is instead of being blinded by what isn't

Gratitude is a simple yet powerful practice. It's a healthful habit endorsed by leaders like the Dalai Lama and backed by solid research. It's no wonder more and more people are embracing it. For most people it's easy to start, and soon, you'll have a treasure trove of uplifting thoughts to turn to whenever you need a boost.

When you take the time to notice the little things in your life, you become more optimistic by default. You choose to focus on the positive aspects of your life and lessen the influence of negative feelings. Even if these beautiful things in your life might already be circulating in your subconscious, putting them down on paper makes them more concrete.

Maintaining a journal enables you to be aware of your own personal accomplishments. Let's face it: We all love to feel appreciated, so it's important to invest in yourself daily. It has been demonstrated that expressing thankfulness lowers social comparisons and decreases the likelihood of resentment toward others. According to a 2014 study, grateful athletes reported higher levels of self-esteem and greater confidence in their ability to trust others.

You can get much better sleep if you take a few minutes before bed to write down a few things for which you are grateful, so ditch those sleeping tablets! You are far less likely to dwell on your worries, freeing your mind for a restful night's sleep. Reflecting on the pleasant things that happened during the day or reminding yourself of what you are grateful for is conducive to relaxation and REMS!

By expressing thankfulness, you are acknowledging the positive aspects of your life. By putting these things down on paper, you can cultivate great relationships, enjoy beautiful experiences, and feel more positive emotions. This is a surefire way to lead a happier life!

Grateful people tend to take better care of themselves, which results in longer lifespans and improved stress levels. Researchers have discovered that concentrating on happy emotions automatically reduces anxiety, makes you feel much more rooted, and gives you more resilience to handle life's ups and downs.

> Collecting Moments is conducive to relaxation and REMS!

I will now tell you just a bit about myself because I think it's essential for you to know where I came from. When I was younger, I had a motorcycle accident, which eventually led to my left leg being amputated. That is a very long story, condensed extremely short.

Trust me! Fast forward a few years and three daughters later, my husband Dave had only just turned fifty-five when he died of cancer. Notice I haven't included a capital 'C' in cancer. This is because I don't want to label cancer as being important in my life; it doesn't deserve it. Unfortunately, Dave was no longer with us when our middle daughter married. However, he had written the 'Father of the Bride' speech, which I proudly gave at her wedding (although I found it extremely difficult to speak his words). It was a bittersweet occasion when our first granddaughter came along. She is a beautiful little girl, but sadly, Dave will never get to hold her.

Today, I have several health complications, and because of this, I am now in a wheelchair. I also have Myoclonic seizures (a type of epilepsy). However, I still live independently and manage my own life. Yes, I struggle some days, but doesn't everyone have days like these? I'm **not** trying to make you feel sorry for me; I'm trying to show you that whatever situation life throws your way, you can always find something to be grateful for. Read that again: **'Whatever situation life throws your way, you can always find something to be grateful for'**. It would help to keep this mantra at the back of your mind: say it, write it down and stick it on your mirror. But above all, remind yourself daily. It really will make things a lot easier.

For many men and women, developing a regular practice of appreciating the little things in life might be one of the most challenging things to do, especially if you're new to journalling. However, this book offers plenty of advice to help you get started. Once you understand what's required, practising Gratitude (which I call 'Collecting Moments') will become second nature, and that's when you' will **really** begin to notice the benefits in your everyday life.

Practising Gratitude = Collecting Moments

Whatever situation life throws my way, I can always find something to be grateful for.

Did you know that, on average, it takes more than two months before a new daily behaviour becomes automatic? In a study published in a renowned social psychology magazine, a health psychology researcher and her team discovered that, on average, it takes sixty-six days. Although I have incorporated the 'sixty-six days' concept into this journal, it's optional if you want to follow it. However, it will help cement the daily Collection of Moments into your life, going forward.

Less scrolling, more living

Another way to build the Collecting Moments habit into your life is to identify a current habit you already do each day and then attach (or stack) your Collecting Moments Journal on top, rather than pairing your journal with a particular time and location. This is called habit stacking. By linking your Collected Moments to a cycle already built into your brain, you make it more likely that you'll stick to the new way of thinking. This can be used to design an obvious cue for nearly any habit you can name.

The habit stacking formula is:

After/Before [ESTABLISHED HABIT], I will write in my 'Collect Moments, Not Things'.

For example:

After I pour my coffee each morning, I will Collect My Moments.
Before I check my email, I will Collect My Moments.
After dinner, I will Collect My Moments.
Before I go running, I will Collect My Moments.

> The ancient Chinese philosopher Lao-Tzu wrote: "Be content with what you have, rejoice in the way things are. When you realise there is nothing lacking, the whole world belongs to you".

The second part of this book highlights some examples of things you should consider with several exercises before you embark on your Collecting Moments journey. Then, when you feel ready, turn to the journal pages in part three and start writing. At the end of every seven days, you will find a Reflection page where you can sum-up how things are going.

You will also find tips, fresh daily positive affirmations, and activities that provide inspirational ideas. These break up the journal pages to prevent slipping back into the old ways of thinking.

I am a Christian now, but please don't let this fact discourage you from your Collecting Moments journey. Whether you're religious or not, this book is for you! It's written for men and women who want to improve their lives. So, go ahead, pick it up and give it a try! In this journal I will use the words The Universe; please feel free to substitute it for whoever/whatever deity you show your appreciation to.

If you miss a day, don't be too hard on yourself and **please** don't give up. Just pick up where you left off some other time, without pressure. Making this journal a chore is the last thing you want to do. Be truthful to yourself; write how you really feel. Don't go around with a painted smile on your face.

If you're happy, by all means, do a happy dance; however, if you're sad, find something you are grateful for and write about it. You'll be surprised how quickly this simple act will lift your spirits.

If it gets really tough and you feel like you're spiralling down a big black hole, it might mean that you are suffering from depression. So pop along to see your Doctor. Poor mental health doesn't have the stigma attached to it as it once did. If you're struggling, talk to your Doctor and/or friends and family.

It's crucial to remember that you can reap the rewards of thankfulness without devoting a lot of time to writing or maintaining an elaborate diary. With this simple Collecting Moments Journal, you can start promoting positivity even if you only have five minutes to spare! Remember....

To begin, take a few minutes to consider what you believe the title of this book means, and jot down a few notes about your thoughts.

o————————————————————————o

o————————————————————————o

o————————————————————————o

o————————————————————————o

o————————————————————————o

If you purchased this book for yourself, what drew you to it? What were your original intentions? If it was a gift, why do you think it was given to you?

o————————————————————————o

o————————————————————————o

o————————————————————————o

o————————————————————————o

o————————————————————————o

Write a list of 10 things that make you smile (and **only** 10). They don't have to cost much, and free is even better. Give yourself 10 points if it is free, 5 points if it costs someone else money and 3 points if it cost you money. We'll do this exercise again in a few weeks to see if your values change.

Positive Affirmations

Write a list of positive affirmations, if you are stuck or don't know any, look on the internet. You can even change the wording, making them personal to you.

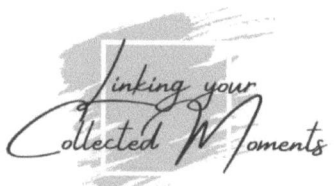

Linking your Collected Moments

Write a list of the things you do every day. Then in the checkbox put a tick if it's suitable to link your journal. Or a cross if it isn't. Now you need to consider which already established habit you want to link it to and why (the 'why' makes you think about the new habit and creates a firmer link between the established habit and the Collecting Moments habit). There's a second page should you need it.

Catch the bus to work	☒
Go to bed LINK THIS - BEFORE I SLEEP	☑
Before taking the dog for a walk	☑
	☐
	☐
	☐
	☐
	☐
	☐
	☐

Examples

It's important to appreciate other people

It's also important for us to notice when other people say thank you.

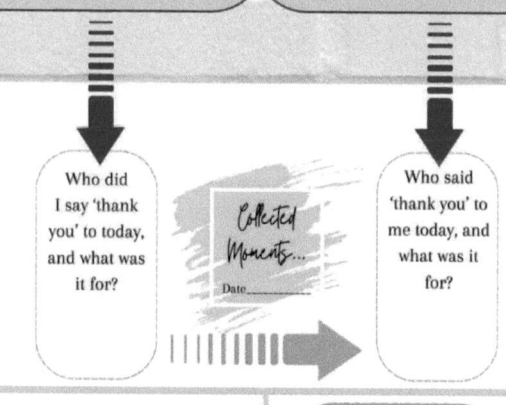

Who did I say 'thank you' to today, and what was it for?

Collected Moments...
Date_____

Who said 'thank you' to me today, and what was it for?

Here are three things I am grateful for today, along with the reasons why.

1

How was my mood today? If it wasn't great, what can I release back to the Universe tomorrow?

Send something back to The Universe to make room for something better tomorrow.

Why are you encouraged to write **why** you are grateful? This establishes a firmer link to your emotions. Next month, you may look back at this page and get the same warm fuzzy feeling when reading it.

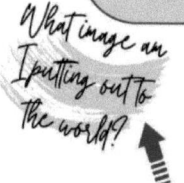

What image am I putting out to the world?

Fresh Daily Affirmation

Collected Moments...
Date 25/5/2024

Who did I say 'thank you' to today, and what was it for?

To the postman for my letters.

Who said 'thank you' to me today, and what was it for?

My Mum when I did the washing up

Here are three things I am grateful for today, along with the reasons why.

1. *My morning cup of coffee - can't function without that kick of caffeine!* ☺
2. *A toddler waving to me on the bus, reminded me how uncomplicated life should be.*
3. *The bulbs in the garden are coming up, come Summer they will be beautiful.*

How was my mood today? If it wasn't great, what can I release back to The Universe to make tomorrow better?

I need to let go of worrying about my job interviews and let The Universe decide.

What image am I putting out to the world?

Collected Moments Tracker

		1	2	3	4	5	6	7
WEEK ONE	Date:	○	○	○	○	○	○	○

		8	9	10	11	12	13	14
WEEK TWO	Date:	○	○	○	○	○	○	○

		15	16	17	18	19	20	21
WEEK THREE	Date:	○	○	○	○	○	○	○

		22	23	24	25	26	27	28
WEEK FOUR	Date:	○	○	○	○	○	○	○

		29	30	31	32	33	34	35
WEEK FIVE	Date:	○	○	○	○	○	○	○

Notes...
_____
_____

		36	37	38	39	40	41	42
WEEK SIX	Date:	○	○	○	○	○	○	○

		43	44	45	46	47	48	49
WEEK SEVEN	Date:	○	○	○	○	○	○	○

		50	51	52	53	54	55	56
WEEK EIGHT	Date:	○	○	○	○	○	○	○

		57	58	59	60	61	62	63
WEEK NINE	Date:	○	○	○	○	○	○	○

	64	65	66
NEARLY THERE!	○	○	⭐

Notes...

_____

_____

Who did I say 'thank you' to today, and what was it for?

Date_____

Who said 'thank you' to me today, and what was it for?

Here are three things I am grateful for today, along with the reasons why.

1 _____
_____

2 _____
_____

3 _____
_____

How was my mood today? If it wasn't great, what can I release back to The Universe to make tomorrow better?

○_____○
○_____○
○_____○

I will be kinder to myself

Who did I say 'thank you' to today, and what was it for?

Collected Moments...
Date_____

Who said 'thank you' to me today, and what was it for?

Here are three things I am grateful for today, along with the reasons why.

1 _____

2 _____

3 _____

How was my mood today? If it wasn't great, what can I release back to The Universe to make tomorrow better?

○_____
○_____
○_____

I won't forget to have fun

Who did I say 'thank you' to today, and what was it for?

Date_____

Who said 'thank you' to me today, and what was it for?

Here are three things I am grateful for today, along with the reasons why.

1 _____
_____

2 _____
_____

3 _____
_____

How was my mood today? If it wasn't great, what can I release back to The Universe to make tomorrow better?

○—————————○

○—————————○

○—————————○

Jobs fill my pockets, adventures fill my soul

| Who did I say 'thank you' to today, and what was it for? |  *Collected Moments...* Date_____ | Who said 'thank you' to me today, and what was it for? |

Here are three things I am grateful for today, along with the reasons why.

1
_____
_____

2
_____
_____

3
_____
_____

How was my mood today? If it wasn't great, what can I release back to The Universe to make tomorrow better?

o———————————o

o———————————o

o———————————o

Which is worse—failing or never trying?

Who did I say 'thank you' to today, and what was it for?

Collected Moments...

Date_____

Who said 'thank you' to me today, and what was it for?

Here are three things I am grateful for today, along with the reasons why.

1
_____
_____

2
_____
_____

3
_____
_____

How was my mood today? If it wasn't great, what can I release back to The Universe to make tomorrow better?

o—————————o

o—————————o

o—————————o

Do I care too much about what others think of me?

Who did I say 'thank you' to today, and what was it for?

Collected Moments...
Date_____

Who said 'thank you' to me today, and what was it for?

Here are three things I am grateful for today, along with the reasons why.

1 _____

2 _____

3 _____

How was my mood today? If it wasn't great, what can I release back to The Universe to make tomorrow better?

o——————————o

o——————————o

o——————————o

There are no shortcuts to any place worth going to

Who did I say 'thank you' to today, and what was it for?

Date_____

Who said 'thank you' to me today, and what was it for?

Here are three things I am grateful for today, along with the reasons why.

1 _____
_____

2 _____
_____

3 _____
_____

How was my mood today? If it wasn't great, what can I release back to The Universe to make tomorrow better?

○ _____
○ _____
○ _____

I try to take my interests and make them my work.

Date_____

What am I most proud of this week?

_____

_____

_____

How do I feel my Collecting Moments journey is progressing?

_____

_____

_____

What could have gone better this week and how can I improve it going forward?

o————————o

o————————o

o————————o

o————————o

o————————o

I didn't come this far to only come this far

Who did I say 'thank you' to today, and what was it for?

Date_____

Who said 'thank you' to me today, and what was it for?

Here are three things I am grateful for today, along with the reasons why.

1 _____
_____

2 _____
_____

3 _____
_____

How was my mood today? If it wasn't great, what can I release back to The Universe to make tomorrow better?

o_____o

o_____o

o_____o

I am excited for the future

Collected Moments...

Date_____

Who did I say 'thank you' to today, and what was it for?	Who said 'thank you' to me today, and what was it for?

Here are three things I am grateful for today, along with the reasons why.

1 _____
_____

2 _____
_____

3 _____
_____

How was my mood today? If it wasn't great, what can I release back to The Universe to make tomorrow better?

o_____o
o_____o
o_____o

Difficult roads often lead to beautiful destinations

Who did I say 'thank you' to today, and what was it for?

Date_____

Who said 'thank you' to me today, and what was it for?

Here are three things I am grateful for today, along with the reasons why.

1 _____
_____

2 _____
_____

3 _____
_____

How was my mood today? If it wasn't great, what can I release back to The Universe to make tomorrow better?

o——————————o

o——————————o

o——————————o

Tough times don't last tough people do!

Who did I say 'thank you' to today, and what was it for?

Collected Moments...

Date_____

Who said 'thank you' to me today, and what was it for?

Here are three things I am grateful for today, along with the reasons why.

1 _____
_____

2 _____
_____

3 _____
_____

How was my mood today? If it wasn't great, what can I release back to The Universe to make tomorrow better?

o_____o

o_____o

o_____o

What image am I putting out to the world?

Who did I say 'thank you' to today, and what was it for?

Date_____

Who said 'thank you' to me today, and what was it for?

Here are three things I am grateful for today, along with the reasons why.

1 _____
   _____

2 _____
   _____

3 _____
   _____

How was my mood today? If it wasn't great, what can I release back to The Universe to make tomorrow better?

○——————————○
○——————————○
○——————————○

I deserve to feel safe and loved

37

Date_____

Who did I say 'thank you' to today, and what was it for?

Who said 'thank you' to me today, and what was it for?

Here are three things I am grateful for today, along with the reasons why.

1
_____
_____

2
_____
_____

3
_____
_____

How was my mood today? If it wasn't great, what can I release back to The Universe to make tomorrow better?

○——————————○

○——————————○

○——————————○

I refuse to give up

Who did I say 'thank you' to today, and what was it for?

Date_____

Who said 'thank you' to me today, and what was it for?

Here are three things I am grateful for today, along with the reasons why.

1 _____
_____

2 _____
_____

3 _____
_____

How was my mood today? If it wasn't great, what can I release back to The Universe to make tomorrow better?

o_____
o_____
o_____

I am enough

Date_____

What am I most proud of this week?

_____

_____

_____

How do I feel my Collecting Moments journey is progressing?

_____

_____

_____

_____

What could have gone better this week and how can I improve it going forward?

o————————o

o————————o

o————————o

o————————o

o————————o

What am I not ready to change yet?

Food For Thought!

A single act of kindness can go a long, long way...

Researchers in positive psychology discovered that a single, intentional act of appreciation resulted in an instantaneous 10% improvement in happiness and a 35% decrease in depressive symptoms. The positive benefits subsided in three to six months, demonstrating that practising thankfulness is an action that should be practised over and over again.

Don't wait; start today by saying "thank you" or letting someone special know how much they mean to you are little but meaningful acts of gratitude that make a big difference.

Collected Moments...

Date_____

Who did I say 'thank you' to today, and what was it for?

Who said 'thank you' to me today, and what was it for?

Here are three things I am grateful for today, along with the reasons why.

1 _____
_____

2 _____
_____

3 _____
_____

How was my mood today? If it wasn't great, what can I release back to The Universe to make tomorrow better?

o─────────o

o─────────o

o─────────o

I never regret something that made me smile

42

> Who did I say 'thank you' to today, and what was it for?

Date_____

> Who said 'thank you' to me today, and what was it for?

Here are three things I am grateful for today, along with the reasons why.

1. _____
   _____

2. _____
   _____

3. _____
   _____

How was my mood today? If it wasn't great, what can I release back to The Universe to make tomorrow better?

○──────────────○

○──────────────○

○──────────────○

The happiest people don't have everything they make the best of everything

Who did I say 'thank you' to today, and what was it for?

Collected Moments...

Date_____

Who said 'thank you' to me today, and what was it for?

Here are three things I am grateful for today, along with the reasons why.

1 _____
_____

2 _____
_____

3 _____
_____

How was my mood today? If it wasn't great, what can I release back to The Universe to make tomorrow better?

o_____o

o_____o

o_____o

I am proud of how hard I am working

44

Who did I say 'thank you' to today, and what was it for?

Collected Moments...

Date_____

Who said 'thank you' to me today, and what was it for?

Here are three things I am grateful for today, along with the reasons why.

1 _____
_____

2 _____
_____

3 _____
_____

How was my mood today? If it wasn't great, what can I release back to The Universe to make tomorrow better?

o_____o

o_____o

o_____o

Do I take the time to listen to others?

Who did I say 'thank you' to today, and what was it for?

Collected Moments...

Date _____

Who said 'thank you' to me today, and what was it for?

Here are three things I am grateful for today, along with the reasons why.

1. _____
   _____

2. _____
   _____

3. _____
   _____

How was my mood today? If it wasn't great, what can I release back to The Universe to make tomorrow better?

o────────o

o────────o

o────────o

A good laugh and a long sleep are the best cures

| Who did I say 'thank you' to today, and what was it for? |  Collected Moments... Date_____ | Who said 'thank you' to me today, and what was it for? |

Here are three things I am grateful for today, along with the reasons why.

1 _____
_____

2 _____
_____

3 _____
_____

How was my mood today? If it wasn't great, what can I release back to The Universe to make tomorrow better?

○_____○
○_____○
○_____○

I'm letting go of what my life should look like

47

Who did I say 'thank you' to today, and what was it for?

Date_____

Who said 'thank you' to me today, and what was it for?

Here are three things I am grateful for today, along with the reasons why.

1
_____
_____

2
_____
_____

3
_____
_____

How was my mood today? If it wasn't great, what can I release back to The Universe to make tomorrow better?

o—————————o

o—————————o

o—————————o

I have the power to create change

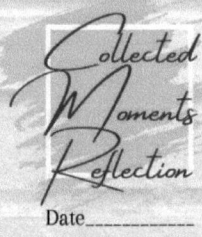

Date_____

What am I most proud of this week?

_____

_____

_____

_____

How do I feel my Collecting Moments journey is progressing?

_____

_____

_____

_____

What could have gone better this week and how can I improve it going forward?

o_____o

o_____o

o_____o

o_____o

o_____o

I am allowed to say no

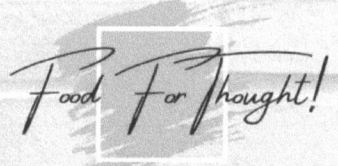

Thanking People Is Beneficial to Businesses

When was the last time you expressed gratitude to a coworker? According to a study by psychologists, a simple "thank you" can make a big difference. Thanking your staff for a job well done can give them a great sense of confidence and self-worth, especially if you are a supervisor. The study also showed that feeling thankful has a cascading impact that boosts coworker trust and encourages more initiative to support one another.

Don't wait: start today and express sincere gratitude to a coworker for their professional contributions.

> Who did I say 'thank you' to today, and what was it for?

Collected Moments...

Date _____

> Who said 'thank you' to me today, and what was it for?

Here are three things I am grateful for today, along with the reasons why.

1. _____
   _____

2. _____
   _____

3. _____
   _____

How was my mood today? If it wasn't great, what can I release back to The Universe to make tomorrow better?

○_____○
○_____○
○_____○

I love what I do and do what I love

Who did I say 'thank you' to today, and what was it for?

Collected Moments...

Date_____

Who said 'thank you' to me today, and what was it for?

Here are three things I am grateful for today, along with the reasons why.

1 _____
_____

2 _____
_____

3 _____
_____

How was my mood today? If it wasn't great, what can I release back to The Universe to make tomorrow better?

o—————————o

o—————————o

o—————————o

I am brave enough to say yes

52

Who did I say 'thank you' to today, and what was it for?

Date_____

Who said 'thank you' to me today, and what was it for?

Here are three things I am grateful for today, along with the reasons why.

1 _____
_____

2 _____
_____

3 _____
_____

How was my mood today? If it wasn't great, what can I release back to The Universe to make tomorrow better?

o_____o

o_____o

o_____o

I am a living, breathing example of motivation

Collected Moments...

Date_____

Who did I say 'thank you' to today, and what was it for?

Who said 'thank you' to me today, and what was it for?

Here are three things I am grateful for today, along with the reasons why.

1

2

3

How was my mood today? If it wasn't great, what can I release back to The Universe to make tomorrow better?

I am living with an abundance of smiles

| Who did I say 'thank you' to today, and what was it for? |  Date_____ | Who said 'thank you' to me today, and what was it for? |

Here are three things I am grateful for today, along with the reasons why.

1 _____
_____

2 _____
_____

3 _____
_____

How was my mood today? If it wasn't great, what can I release back to The Universe to make tomorrow better?

o—————o

o—————o

o—————o

I am inspiring people through my work

Who did I say 'thank you' to today, and what was it for?

Collected Moments...
Date_____

Who said 'thank you' to me today, and what was it for?

Here are three things I am grateful for today, along with the reasons why.

1 _____
_____

2 _____
_____

3 _____
_____

How was my mood today? If it wasn't great, what can I release back to The Universe to make tomorrow better?

Today is a phenomenal day

Who did I say 'thank you' to today, and what was it for?

Date_____

Who said 'thank you' to me today, and what was it for?

Here are three things I am grateful for today, along with the reasons why.

1 _____
_____

2 _____
_____

3 _____
_____

How was my mood today? If it wasn't great, what can I release back to The Universe to make tomorrow better?

o_____o

o_____o

o_____o

I am filled with focus

Date_____

What am I most proud of this week?

_____
_____
_____

How do I feel my Collecting Moments journey is progressing?

_____
_____
_____

What could have gone better this week and how can I improve it going forward?

o————————o
o————————o
o————————o
o————————o
o————————o

I colour my life with good friends and laughter

If at any time you feel you are losing interest or getting bored, read through part one again. You should regain your enthusiasm to continue.

Who did I say 'thank you' to today, and what was it for?

Date_____

Who said 'thank you' to me today, and what was it for?

Here are three things I am grateful for today, along with the reasons why.

1 _____
_____

2 _____
_____

3 _____
_____

How was my mood today? If it wasn't great, what can I release back to The Universe to make tomorrow better?

_____
_____
_____

I am independent and self-sufficient

Who did I say 'thank you' to today, and what was it for?

Collected Moments...
Date_____

Who said 'thank you' to me today, and what was it for?

Here are three things I am grateful for today, along with the reasons why.

1 _____

2 _____

3 _____

How was my mood today? If it wasn't great, what can I release back to The Universe to make tomorrow better?

o_____o

o_____o

o_____o

I can be whatever I want to be

Collected Moments...

Date _____

Who did I say 'thank you' to today, and what was it for?

Who said 'thank you' to me today, and what was it for?

Here are three things I am grateful for today, along with the reasons why.

1. _____
_____

2. _____
_____

3. _____
_____

How was my mood today? If it wasn't great, what can I release back to The Universe to make tomorrow better?

_____
_____
_____

I am not defined by my past I am driven by my future

Who did I say 'thank you' to today, and what was it for?

Collected Moments...
Date_____

Who said 'thank you' to me today, and what was it for?

Here are three things I am grateful for today, along with the reasons why.

1 _____
_____

2 _____
_____

3 _____
_____

How was my mood today? If it wasn't great, what can I release back to The Universe to make tomorrow better?

o―――――――o

o―――――――o

o―――――――o

I use obstacles to motivate me to learn and grow

Who did I say 'thank you' to today, and what was it for?

Collected Moments...
Date_____

Who said 'thank you' to me today, and what was it for?

Here are three things I am grateful for today, along with the reasons why.

1 _____
_____

2 _____
_____

3 _____
_____

How was my mood today? If it wasn't great, what can I release back to The Universe to make tomorrow better?

o————————o

o————————o

o————————o

Today will be a productive day

Who did I say 'thank you' to today, and what was it for?

Date_____

Who said 'thank you' to me today, and what was it for?

Here are three things I am grateful for today, along with the reasons why.

1
_____
_____

2
_____
_____

3
_____
_____

How was my mood today? If it wasn't great, what can I release back to The Universe to make tomorrow better?

o_____o

o_____o

o_____o

I am intelligent and focused

Who did I say 'thank you' to today, and what was it for?

Date _____

Who said 'thank you' to me today, and what was it for?

Here are three things I am grateful for today, along with the reasons why.

1 _____
_____

2 _____
_____

3 _____
_____

How was my mood today? If it wasn't great, what can I release back to The Universe to make tomorrow better?

o————————o
o————————o
o————————o

I am getting healthier every day

67

Date_____

What am I most proud of this week?

_____

_____

_____

How do I feel my Collecting Moments journey is progressing?

_____

_____

_____

What could have gone better this week and how can I improve it going forward?

- _____
- _____
- _____
- _____
- _____

Each and every day I am getting closer to achieving my goals

Food For Thought!

The Power of Gratitude in a Romantic Relationship

Being thankful benefits you personally, but it can also improve your love connections when you are the one receiving it! According to a recent study, individuals reported feeling more happy with their relationship and their partner's responsiveness to their needs after they were shown thankfulness. Six to nine months afterwards, gratitude was still shown to have a lasting impact.

Don't wait: start today, even though getting ready for the day ahead can be stressful in the morning, take the time to express your love and affection for your mate.

Collected Moments...

Date_____

Who did I say 'thank you' to today, and what was it for?

Who said 'thank you' to me today, and what was it for?

Here are three things I am grateful for today, along with the reasons why.

1

2

3

How was my mood today? If it wasn't great, what can I release back to The Universe to make tomorrow better?

I am constantly growing and evolving into a better person

Who did I say 'thank you' to today, and what was it for?

Date _____

Who said 'thank you' to me today, and what was it for?

Here are three things I am grateful for today, along with the reasons why.

1
2
3

How was my mood today? If it wasn't great, what can I release back to The Universe to make tomorrow better?

I am freeing myself from all destructive doubt and fear

Who did I say 'thank you' to today, and what was it for?

Collected Moments...
Date_____

Who said 'thank you' to me today, and what was it for?

Here are three things I am grateful for today, along with the reasons why.

1 _____
_____

2 _____
_____

3 _____
_____

How was my mood today? If it wasn't great, what can I release back to The Universe to make tomorrow better?

o————————o

o————————o

o————————o

I accept myself for who I am

Who did I say 'thank you' to today, and what was it for?

Date_____

Who said 'thank you' to me today, and what was it for?

Here are three things I am grateful for today, along with the reasons why.

1 _____
_____

2 _____
_____

3 _____
_____

How was my mood today? If it wasn't great, what can I release back to The Universe to make tomorrow better?

_____
_____
_____

I am going to forgive myself and set myself free

Who did I say 'thank you' to today, and what was it for?

Collected Moments...

Date_____

Who said 'thank you' to me today, and what was it for?

Here are three things I am grateful for today, along with the reasons why.

1 _____

2 _____

3 _____

How was my mood today? If it wasn't great, what can I release back to The Universe to make tomorrow better?

I am healing and strengthening every day

Who did I say 'thank you' to today, and what was it for?

Date_____

Who said 'thank you' to me today, and what was it for?

Here are three things I am grateful for today, along with the reasons why.

1 _____
_____

2 _____
_____

3 _____
_____

How was my mood today? If it wasn't great, what can I release back to The Universe to make tomorrow better?

o──────────o
o──────────o
o──────────o

I have incredible power within me

Who did I say 'thank you' to today, and what was it for?

Date_____

Who said 'thank you' to me today, and what was it for?

Here are three things I am grateful for today, along with the reasons why.

1
_____
_____

2
_____
_____

3
_____
_____

How was my mood today? If it wasn't great, what can I release back to The Universe to make tomorrow better?

o—————————o

o—————————o

o—————————o

There are people that care about me and my worth

Date_____

What am I most proud of this week?

_____

_____

_____

How do I feel my Collecting Moments journey is progressing?

_____

_____

_____

_____

What could have gone better this week and how can I improve it going forward?

- _____
- _____
- _____
- _____
- _____

My past might be ugly but I am still beautiful

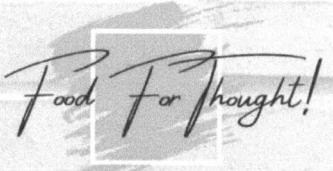

It's never too early...

A psychologist and researcher developed and implemented a gratitude programme, for children ages 8 to 11. Compared to their peers who did not participate, the children who received the lessons demonstrated increased good feelings, appreciation, and thankfulness. Five months following the programme, the differences between the two groups peaked, demonstrating the long-lasting impact of the lessons.

Don't wait: start today by setting a good example and teach young people in your family the value of thankfulness. At your next meal with children, ask them to say something kind to each individual at the table. I promise you'll be moved by the responses!

Who did I say 'thank you' to today, and what was it for?

Date_____

Who said 'thank you' to me today, and what was it for?

Here are three things I am grateful for today, along with the reasons why.

1 _____
_____

2 _____
_____

3 _____
_____

How was my mood today? If it wasn't great, what can I release back to The Universe to make tomorrow better?

○_____
○_____
○_____

I am the change I want to see in the world

Who did I say 'thank you' to today, and what was it for?

Date_____

Who said 'thank you' to me today, and what was it for?

Here are three things I am grateful for today, along with the reasons why.

1

2

3

How was my mood today? If it wasn't great, what can I release back to The Universe to make tomorrow better?

I'm taking baby steps towards a brighter future

Who did I say 'thank you' to today, and what was it for?

Collected Moments...

Date_____

Who said 'thank you' to me today, and what was it for?

Here are three things I am grateful for today, along with the reasons why.

1 _____
_____

2 _____
_____

3 _____
_____
_____

How was my mood today? If it wasn't great, what can I release back to The Universe to make tomorrow better?

○_____○
○_____○
○_____○

Tomorrow tomorrow
I love you
tomorrow

Who did I say 'thank you' to today, and what was it for?

Collected Moments...

Date_____

Who said 'thank you' to me today, and what was it for?

Here are three things I am grateful for today, along with the reasons why.

1 _____
_____

2 _____
_____

3 _____
_____

How was my mood today? If it wasn't great, what can I release back to The Universe to make tomorrow better?

o——————o

o——————o

o——————o

Note to self: I am going to make you so proud

Collected Moments...

Date _____

Who did I say 'thank you' to today, and what was it for?

Who said 'thank you' to me today, and what was it for?

Here are three things I am grateful for today, along with the reasons why.

1. _____
_____

2. _____
_____

3. _____
_____
_____

How was my mood today? If it wasn't great, what can I release back to The Universe to make tomorrow better?

o———————o

o———————o

o———————o

My mistakes do not define me

Who did I say 'thank you' to today, and what was it for?

Collected Moments...

Date_____

Who said 'thank you' to me today, and what was it for?

Here are three things I am grateful for today, along with the reasons why.

1 _____
_____

2 _____
_____

3 _____
_____

How was my mood today? If it wasn't great, what can I release back to The Universe to make tomorrow better?

o—————————o

o—————————o

o—————————o

I finish what matters and let go of what does not

Who did I say 'thank you' to today, and what was it for?

Date _____

Who said 'thank you' to me today, and what was it for?

Here are three things I am grateful for today, along with the reasons why.

1 _____
_____

2 _____
_____

3 _____
_____

How was my mood today? If it wasn't great, what can I release back to The Universe to make tomorrow better?

o—————————o
o—————————o
o—————————o

My life has meaning what I do has meaning.

Date_____

What am I most proud of this week?

_____

_____

_____

How do I feel my Collecting Moments journey is progressing?

_____

_____

_____

What could have gone better this week and how can I improve it going forward?

○────────○

○────────○

○────────○

○────────○

○────────○

I'm doing the best that I can

If at any time you feel you are losing interest or getting bored, read through part one again. You should regain your enthusiasm to continue.

Who did I say 'thank you' to today, and what was it for?

Date_____

Who said 'thank you' to me today, and what was it for?

Here are three things I am grateful for today, along with the reasons why.

1
2
3

How was my mood today? If it wasn't great, what can I release back to The Universe to make tomorrow better?

Happiness is a choice

Who did I say 'thank you' to today, and what was it for?

Collected Moments...
Date_____

Who said 'thank you' to me today, and what was it for?

Here are three things I am grateful for today, along with the reasons why.

1 _____
_____

2 _____
_____

3 _____
_____

How was my mood today? If it wasn't great, what can I release back to The Universe to make tomorrow better?

o————————o

o————————o

o————————o

Every day is full of potential

Who did I say 'thank you' to today, and what was it for?

Date_____

Who said 'thank you' to me today, and what was it for?

Here are three things I am grateful for today, along with the reasons why.

1 _____
_____

2 _____
_____

3 _____
_____

How was my mood today? If it wasn't great, what can I release back to The Universe to make tomorrow better?

○_____
○_____
○_____

I am creative and inspired

Who did I say 'thank you' to today, and what was it for?

Collected Moments...
Date_____

Who said 'thank you' to me today, and what was it for?

Here are three things I am grateful for today, along with the reasons why.

1 _____
_____

2 _____
_____

3 _____
_____

How was my mood today? If it wasn't great, what can I release back to The Universe to make tomorrow better?

o——————————o

o——————————o

o——————————o

Self-care has never been such fun

Who did I say 'thank you' to today, and what was it for?

Date_____

Who said 'thank you' to me today, and what was it for?

Here are three things I am grateful for today, along with the reasons why.

1 _____
_____

2 _____
_____

3 _____
_____

How was my mood today? If it wasn't great, what can I release back to The Universe to make tomorrow better?

o─────────o
o─────────o
o─────────o

Sometimes I win, sometimes I learn

93

Date_____

Who did I say 'thank you' to today, and what was it for?	Who said 'thank you' to me today, and what was it for?

Here are three things I am grateful for today, along with the reasons why.

1 _____

2 _____

3 _____

How was my mood today? If it wasn't great, what can I release back to The Universe to make tomorrow better?

o————————o

o————————o

o————————o

I look at the world as if seeing for the first time

Who did I say 'thank you' to today, and what was it for?

Date_____

Who said 'thank you' to me today, and what was it for?

Here are three things I am grateful for today, along with the reasons why.

1 _____

2 _____

3 _____

How was my mood today? If it wasn't great, what can I release back to The Universe to make tomorrow better?

○——————○
○——————○
○——————○

I create my own calm

Date_____

What am I most proud of this week?

_____

_____

_____

How do I feel my Collecting Moments journey is progressing?

_____

_____

_____

_____

What could have gone better this week and how can I improve it going forward?

o————————o

o————————o

o————————o

o————————o

o————————o

I am a warrior not a worrier

Things that make you smile

Start by jotting down the score you got on page 16 _____, then write a list of 10 things that make you smile now (and **only** 10). They don't have to cost much, and free is even better. As before, give yourself 10 points if it is free, 5 points if it costs someone else money and 3 points if it cost you money. Is there a difference in your score? Have your values changed? What does this tell you? What are your thoughts on this? Write a few words on the next page.

Things that make you smile continued

Who did I say 'thank you' to today, and what was it for?

Date_____

Who said 'thank you' to me today, and what was it for?

Here are three things I am grateful for today, along with the reasons why.

1 _____
_____

2 _____
_____

3 _____
_____

How was my mood today? If it wasn't great, what can I release back to The Universe to make tomorrow better?

○_____○

○_____○

○_____○

I teach myself the art of resting

Who did I say 'thank you' to today, and what was it for?

Collected Moments...
Date_____

Who said 'thank you' to me today, and what was it for?

Here are three things I am grateful for today, along with the reasons why.

1 _____
_____

2 _____
_____

3 _____
_____

How was my mood today? If it wasn't great, what can I release back to The Universe to make tomorrow better?

o————————o

o————————o

o————————o

If not now then when?

100

Who did I say 'thank you' to today, and what was it for?

Collected Moments...
Date_____

Who said 'thank you' to me today, and what was it for?

Here are three things I am grateful for today, along with the reasons why.

1 _____

2 _____

3 _____

How was my mood today? If it wasn't great, what can I release back to The Universe to make tomorrow better?

○——————○

○——————○

○——————○

I take life one day at a time

Who did I say 'thank you' to today, and what was it for?	 Collected Moments... Date_____	Who said 'thank you' to me today, and what was it for?

Here are three things I am grateful for today, along with the reasons why.

How was my mood today? If it wasn't great, what can I release back to The Universe to make tomorrow better?

1. _____
   _____

2. _____
   _____

3. _____
   _____

o———————————o

o———————————o

o———————————o

bloom and grow

Who did I say 'thank you' to today, and what was it for?

Date_____

Who said 'thank you' to me today, and what was it for?

Here are three things I am grateful for today, along with the reasons why.

1 _____
_____

2 _____
_____

3 _____
_____

How was my mood today? If it wasn't great, what can I release back to The Universe to make tomorrow better?

○_____
○_____
○_____

My life is better when I'm laughing

Who did I say 'thank you' to today, and what was it for?

Collected Moments...
Date_____

Who said 'thank you' to me today, and what was it for?

Here are three things I am grateful for today, along with the reasons why.

1
2
3

How was my mood today? If it wasn't great, what can I release back to The Universe to make tomorrow better?

There is sunshine after every storm

104

Who did I say 'thank you' to today, and what was it for?

Collected Moments...

Date_____

Who said 'thank you' to me today, and what was it for?

Here are three things I am grateful for today, along with the reasons why.

1 _____
_____

2 _____
_____

3 _____
_____

How was my mood today? If it wasn't great, what can I release back to The Universe to make tomorrow better?

○_____○

○_____○

○_____○

The quieter I am the more I can listen

Collected Moments Reflection

Date_____

What am I most proud of this week?

_____

_____

_____

How do I feel my Collecting Moments journey is progressing?

_____

_____

_____

_____

What could have gone better this week and how can I improve it going forward?

○────────────○

○────────────○

○────────────○

○────────────○

○────────────○

I don't follow a path I make my own

So what's next...

Day sixty-six is just around the corner so by now you should be an aficionado of gratitude, but don't let all your hard work slip by the wayside. To continue your journey get yourself a notebook or journal and every day record the following:

1. Date
2. Who did you say 'thank you' to, and what was it for?
3. Who said 'thank you' to you, and what was it for?
4. List three things you are grateful for, along with the reasons why.
5. Your overall mood and what you can release back to The Universe.
6. Positive affirmation. Use the list you created on page 17 or recycle the ones in this journal if you are stuck for ideas.

To create a simpler version you only have to add the date and list three things you are grateful for, along with the reasons why. It's entirely up to you.

Why didn't I make this journal last longer than sixty-six days? It was to save you money! More pages would have increased the cost of this book (which is also why it is not in colour). As I want to help as many people as possible to enrich their lives, it made sense to me to make it as economical as possible.

If you have any questions or suggestions, you can email me at collect_moments_not_things@outlook.com

Good luck Collecting Moments,

Love Katie H   X

Katie H

Who did I say 'thank you' to today, and what was it for?

Date_____

Who said 'thank you' to me today, and what was it for?

Here are three things I am grateful for today, along with the reasons why.

1 _____
_____

2 _____
_____

3 _____
_____

How was my mood today? If it wasn't great, what can I release back to The Universe to make tomorrow better?

○—————————○
○—————————○
○—————————○

Life is a song and I sing

109

Who did I say 'thank you' to today, and what was it for?

Date_____

Who said 'thank you' to me today, and what was it for?

Here are three things I am grateful for today, along with the reasons why.

1 _____
_____

2 _____
_____

3 _____
_____

How was my mood today? If it wasn't great, what can I release back to The Universe to make tomorrow better?

o————————o

o————————o

o————————o

My home is a sanctuary I fill it with peace

Day sixty-six

Collected Moments...

Date _____

Who did I say 'thank you' to today, and what was it for?

Who said 'thank you' to me today, and what was it for?

Here are three things I am grateful for today, along with the reasons why.

1. _____
   _____

2. _____
   _____

3. _____
   _____

How was my mood today? If it wasn't great, what can I release back to The Universe to make tomorrow better?

○——————————○
○——————————○
○——————————○

I've fallen in love with me!

This is just the beginning...

About the Author:

Kate Hadley is a recovering Traffic Warden!

Kate, the daughter of an American father and English mother, was born in Reading, Berkshire, England, in 1957. She has had a varied employment history, including being a Traffic Warden for Merseyside Police, when she proudly booked The Stranglers, Ted Rogers (from 3-2-1 Dusty Bin fame), and a bright yellow Rolls Royce to name but a few; Kate draws on her extensive experience working for Future Publishing, where she was promoted to Senior Disk Editor. Writing and designing have always been her passions, and her remarkable style is echoed in the unique books she creates. Kate has three daughters, is Widowed and lives near Bath, England, with her two cats!

Printed by Libri Plureos GmbH in Hamburg, Germany